Orbit

Poems by

Megeen R. Mulholland

Finishing Line Press
Georgetown, Kentucky

Orbit

*To Rauri and Maura,
Stars of the County Down*

Copyright © 2018 by Megeen R. Mulholland
ISBN 978-1-63534-412-7 First Edition
All rights reserved under International and Pan-American Copyright Conventions. No part of this book may be reproduced in any manner whatsoever without written permission from the publisher, except in the case of brief quotations embodied in critical articles and reviews.

ACKNOWLEDGMENTS

Grateful acknowledgement is made to the following publications in which some of these poems first appeared:

"Borders," *The Sweet Annie & Sweet Pea Review*
"Maternity," "Laundry Day," *Women Writers: A Zine*
"My Mother's Signals," *The Seattle Review*
"Harvest," *Barkeater: The Adirondack Review*
"Measuring the Ingredients," *Connecticut River Review*
 "Honeymoon," *Phoebe: Journal of Feminist Scholarship, Theory, and Aesthetics*
"Hobby," *Blueline*
"Buoy," *Modern Language Studies*
"Charity," *U.S. Catholic*
"First Illness," *Mothers Always Write*
"Leave Taking," *Mom Writer's Literary Magazine*

Publisher: Leah Maines
Editor: Christen Kincaid
Interior Photos: Author's Personal Collection
Cover Art: Murial H. Mulholland, Author's Personal Collection
Author Photo: Denis G. Mulholland, Author's Personal Collection
Cover Design: Elizabeth Maines McCleavy

Printed in the USA on acid-free paper.
Order online: www.finishinglinepress.com
         also available on amazon.com

Author inquiries and mail orders:
Finishing Line Press
P. O. Box 1626
Georgetown, Kentucky 40324
U. S. A.

Table of Contents

Borders 1

Maternity Ward 3

Maternity 4

Picnic 6

My Mother's Signals 7

Harvest 8

Measuring the Ingredients 9

Laundry Day 10

Rose Fever 11

Honeymoon 13

Hobby 14

Buoy 15

Here She Is 16

Esther Williams 17

One of Us 18

Charity 20

Dear Mom 22

Who Can Say? 24

First Illness 26

Leave Taking 28

Well, Well, Well 30

Orbit 32

Borders

Within the borders
of the photograph
the little girl
and her governess
form a contrast
as the young girl
wears a white pressed dress
edged with lace
at her neck, elbows, and knees
while her governess
wears black—
her dark hair knotted neatly
beneath her pleated cap,
her square collar
tight around her neck,
holding her head straight
above her stiffened shoulders,
the wrap of dark fabric
falling down to her wrists,
buttoning in her narrow bodice,
the dark skirt draping
her laced ankles
just above her
thick-soled shoes.

In a repeated sequence
the girl sits boldly
on a small swing,
her plait tumbling
from the wind-blown bow,
as her fingers curl
loosely around either rope,
and her ankles gently
cross over each other,
the buckles shining in mid air
as my great aunt pushes her—
her own heels sinking deeper
into the soil she stands on,
imprinting her position
behind the girl who glides
forward and above,

gaining momentum from
her stationary nanny
who stays so close behind,
she risks impact with the girl
as she pushes her steadily on,
extending her arms ever outward
toward the child,
ready to catch her
should she fall.

Maternity Ward

Jaundice

Induced

Edema

Nuchal cord

Cyanosis

Breech Presentation

Chloasma

Postpartum Depression

Maternity

I bought a little black dress
with you in mind, today, Mother,
with you as my inspiration—
my model, my idol, the best-dressed
expectant woman of all time.

I still pore over the photographs
of you, taken by your most ardent admirer,
my father, in the glory of your last
trimester with each child, and
still can't get over the ensembles
you pulled together even then—
the lace tunics, velvet wraps, clutch purses, and
never ending array of scarves and shoes.

It seems you always had somewhere to go,
off arm-in-arm with Dad,
who was eager to show you off—
his bride, his wife, the mother of his awaited child, his lifelong love.

I have always been less glamorous
than you, who I so marveled at,
more hesitant to reveal myself
through the fiber of my own clothes.

But I went to a maternity shop
like you used to urge my sisters to do
and looked through the racks, searching out
the midriff panel you relied on
for support, all those years,
underneath it all.

I had trouble at first,
amid the trendy low-cut fashions,
finding garments that would
help me display your blend
of modesty and confidence.

I was only browsing
when I saw the little black dress
hanging there, a wink of fabric

beckoning me.

When I got it into the dressing room,
I saw it was a black v-neck slip
of a dress, shirred at the sleeves
and skirt hem. I slid it over my head
and watched it cling to my body
all the way down as it fell over me—
accentuating my breasts, belly, and hips,
each part at once my most prominent feature,
in an assured pronouncement of womanhood.

When I stepped out to look
in the three-way mirror,
the shopkeeper, who had before
been moving subtly between rack and counter,
in an attempt not to follow or bother,
began to dote on me, adjust and smooth
the shoulders, say how much
she liked the dress since it had arrived,
pointed out the material would grow with me
as my pregnancy progressed.

I don't need it.
I don't know where I will wear it.
But as I imagined your expression
of approval, I knew I had to have it,
if only to pass down a summer snapshot
of me in it to my own child—
this is how I wore my pride
when I carried you, Little One,
this is how my mother
taught me.

Picnic

calico

strawberries

kaiser roll

honeybee

family

My Mother's Signals

I remember the dinner whistle calling us
from just-dim games
with the green-house neighbors
from down the hill,
home to the picnic
set out in summer
on redwood benches—
salads and a cake
for my birthday sister,

the dinner whistle calling us
from the stream and thistles
behind our house
from over the hill,
home to potpies—
edges browned and crimped
like the fallen leaves,

the dinner whistle
penetrating our igloo—
closed in with mounds of snow,
our mother had only to open the patio door,
and Alaska would vanish—
our clothes, on the boot mat, would melt
as the bread and stew steamed,

the whistle rebounding the mountains
in the bare growth of spring,
and ringing me in—
away from other friendships,
as that year I longed for my ear
only to hear the kids' voices
disclosing evening secrets
about others our age—
my own shame calling out
again and again,
until I'd do myself in,
responding to my mother's signals
saying, come home,
I've an early melon
for you, just sliced from the vine.

Harvest

She'd come to the garden by bicycle—
her wire basket tipping
with the solid-skinned squash
she'd heaved from its leaves,
her breath weighing
full as the moonlight—
falling as if all of October
would come down before
one more gathering
in the garden—
bare as her hands.

She dug for the potatoes—
found them heavy and round,
limping from the earth
like soft-shelled turtles—
one eye at a time,
then withdrawn into her pockets.
Under the browning and bitter greens
she found the carrots nested
like whole yellow mice
curled in wet thin fur,
nestling her fingers
as she collected stray radish
from the frost—
each one pulsing red in her palm.

And as she steadied the basket,
gripping the handle bars,
placing her feet over the pedals,
and coaxing the swollen tires
slowly from the dirt
scarred with stones,
she was unsteady on the road—
until the weight of her labor
settled forward together,
and her harvest
pulled her down
the hard-packed hill
toward home.

Measuring the Ingredients

Measuring the ingredients,
sprinkling spices into the pot
like dust, her handwriting
on the recipe card blurs.
So this is when I begin to cry.
I look at the solid cast
of the iron pot,
rub the dark patina
as if it could grant a wish.
Even the largest pans
in our house overflowed,
unable to hold the
contents of her creation.
We clattered to our chairs
before we were called,
heaped our plates as if famished—
we scooped, speared, and relished,
complimenting our mother
with full, silent mouths,
our intermittent murmuring
coaxing her into her chair,
always the last to sit down
at her own decorated table.
In the midst of her company,
the air saturated with
the rising vapors of
the feast and blessing
that moved among us like guests,
it seemed those meals
would go on forever,
every one of us handing
a salver on to the next
in an endless passing
of each course, passing on,
passing on, an eternal passing.

Laundry Day

On laundry day,
my mother would plant her feet
at the sodden base of the stem
of our rotating clothesline
and clothespin my father's slacks
into place, one pair after another,
until they swayed together
like filaments of a flower,
the belt loops protruding
from the waist tops like anther,
soft lint pollinating
the air around her.

Again and again
she'd stoop to unfold
from her woven basket
pillowcases, dish towels, and blouses
that unfurled like ecstatic petals,
blossoming in her chafed hands—
a hovering bluster of color
as she hung and adjusted them
one by one, arranging her bouquet.

As she'd turn the line
on its fragile creaking style,
the bloomers ballooned
into overly anxious ovules
quivering with anticipation
above a half-slip calyx,
the baby's stringed bibs
forming the spreading sepals
at the center of it all.

At last, my mother would stand
straight and step back, hands on hips,
as if to gain perspective
on her creation,
drink in the scent of it,
and watch the wind
deliver it over
to the sky
with a flourish.

Rose Fever

When my mother said
I must have inherited
Rose Fever
from my father,
I wanted to sneeze
forever, experience
the uncontrollable
elation of each
spontaneous release
until the water
streaming from my eyes
became tears.

I'd look forward to June
when the bountiful weeds,
having sprung forth
just weeks before
produced luscious buds
I'd protect from wind and harm,
nurturing the pollen all season,
cultivating my own
little piece of Heaven,
whispering their names
in earnest, like a prayer—
sumac glabra, solidago rigida, ambrosia artemisiifolia.

Mid summer, I'd scour the fields
with outstretched hands,
brush the golden heads
with keen fingertips,
enfold the flowering spikes,
and feel the scarlet dust
settle at the center of my palms
while the spores rose

above in a winged mist
of sun struck angels who
I'd guide toward my face
like a newly baptized believer,
overcome with the spirit.

Breathe it in!
Breathe it in!
Breathe it all in!
Each inhalation,
I imagined, took
me higher, up
to Father who
floated far above
his youngest daughter—
awaiting my arrival.

I'd breathe in as
deeply as I could,
holding my breath
until the burning
in my lungs forced
me to exhale—
only to find myself
still standing still,
bound to the land
he had left us.

My eyes itching,
chest heaving,
throat closing,
I'd begin to run—
blind and faltering,
released on to and
entangled in the wild
field of our backyard,

clutching at the stalks
on my way down,
attempting to seize
upon the strength of
those unyielding roots.

Honeymoon

I know these are from their honeymoon in New England. My mother poses on an empty trolley car in a dark scoop-neck blouse, wide striped skirt, and sling-back flats. Her mound of blond hair is gathered on top of her head, and a bracelet dangles from her wrist above her wedding ring. She smiles even though she has had enough. *When are we going back to the shore?* But her husband cannot detach himself from the lure of railway cars. They have been abandoned in a field, great ferns and weeds grow in where the passengers once sat. The windows have been damaged by the elements, and the double doors are warped wide open. Yet my father carries his fare. He aims at my mother, poised at the controls with pointed toe. *What is the attraction?* She does not notice what rises above as he entreats her to grace the threshold of the end car destined *SPECIAL*.

Hobby

No one asked me about my father until the second grade. Then I told them he was an engineer and, more proudly, that he was dead. Not out of cruelty, but morbid honor, for I knew it would set me apart from every one of them.

Together we composed for him a figure with the strength and vigor of *The Little Engine That Could*, and the gentle sympathy of *Mike Mulligan and Mary Ann*. I joined the conjecture about whether he could see or hear us, and what he would think. I considered him a kind judge, but other kids were scared of his omnipresent power, even though I said it was only meant to protect. They had to give me the last word, but alone in the girls' room, I'd kneel on the tiles and pray for his return so I could prove I knew him best.

From the boxes of tiny trains hidden in the cellar, and the faded photos of railway cars still pinned up in the workshop, I gathered that he had been a careful conductor, guiding his cars out to the rails in the morning, and leading them safely again into the station at night. My mother once told me he had called me his *little caboose* as he rocked me in his arms days before he died.

Another parent asked her child what railroad he had worked for, and I asked my mother in turn. She shook her head with a grimace of dismay and said, no, he was a civil engineer who designed the roads spanning our county—trains were just his hobby.

Shortly after, when we studied systems of transportation in school, I also learned the caboose was a detachable car, often uncoupled to lighten the load of a streamliner so it can proceed unencumbered to its final destination.

Buoy

Below deck,
my father has taken
a picture of the bow,
and his tokens float
across the photo
like life buoys
ringing out to me—
I know those books,
that shuffled deck of cards,
this compass, key, and pen,
his first snapshot of my mother.
I have watched her many times
arrange these mementos
since his death,
plotting them out
on top of his desk
like points on a map,
charting their journey,
searching for the wayward turn
while staring at her own picture—
holding herself in the palm of her hands—
smiling out at him
as he tries to frame her
against the unsteady horizon—
her blue eyes wide
despite the blinding rays,
the sunburn on her shoulders
singeing her blond waves,
her smile, at once
assured and wary,
bordering on disbelief
as if she realizes,
with the release
of the shutter,
she has stumbled
upon treasure.

Here She Is

Here she is *all dolled up* on the arm of Eddie Harms. Here she is, in a hat with a feather, in a foursome at dinner with Alfred Thomas, the prospective *doctor*. Here she's crushing her corsage, hugging Earl Mattson, the unassuming boy next door who, *to no one's surprise*, became a quiet hero in the war, his chest laden with medals as he grins against the backdrop of the Memorial Day parade. Here she is in a swing coat and high heels with Jerry Vale, they called him *Sonny* then, her protective arm around the shoulder of the sentimental crooner whom she'd known since he was just a kid. In this one, a stocky figure has his arm around her, and although her pose endures, her gaze falls beyond the focus of the lens. Oh, so this must be *the man she almost married* to please Grandpa, though not one of us can even remember his name. And here she is, at last, with my father, the one who captured her, carrying her sandals on the beach, barefoot in *Shangri-La* where nobody ever saw her happier, her smile before the sepia horizon outshining the sun.

Esther Williams

Summers after
my father died,
we'd call my mother "Esther"—
the way she would glide
through the water
rolling from shoulder to shoulder,
her arms poised in the air
like sparkling wands,
performing the backstroke
as graceful as a movie star.

Her fingertips and flutter kick
created ripples as she swam,
the sun catching the glimmer
of the waves that encircled her,
holding her up like a brilliant supporting cast,
changing into any formation at her every whim.

She wore her swim cap
like a kind of crown,
the moist, supple, colored flowers
falling over her ear or brow
so she'd appear as my glossy heroine,
saturated with all the glamour
her child's eyes could hold.

Like a Hollywood marathon,
scenes from *Easy to Love* or *Pagan Love Song*,
she did not emerge from the pool all season—
we'd wake to find her there,
repeatedly immersing herself,
first in the tepid shallows
before plunging, by afternoon,
far into the deep end,

and eventually resurfacing,
sustaining herself all evening
in a back float, face up,
looking toward the heavens
as if imagining his
way of life there,
weightless.

One of Us

The one of us
in front of the birch trees
she said, is the one where
I am expecting you.

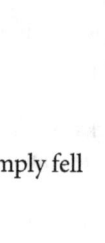

I found it finally,
after months of searching
attic boxes filled with mementos
of my siblings' births before me,
when an unfinished baby book simply fell
open to this image I've coveted
ever since she spoke the words.

It is early evening,
and the night lies before us—
my father, in a dark suit, white shirt, solid tie,
stands slightly angled, eyeing
the timer through his smile.

My mother stands straight on,
with the weight on her back leg,
her opposite front toe poised,
in a skirt set of black lace
with scalloped fringe,
a velvet stole hanging
from her forearm
while my father's hand
wraps her shoulder.

Her hair is coiffed,
her red lips parted,
a short linked earring dangles
beneath one of her curls,

and only her purse is awry
as she holds her clutch
with one hand before her abdomen,
squinting due to the glimmer of her ring
caught in the setting sun.

Between the two of them
the narrow white birches are young,
unable to stand upright alone,
they are tethered with cord
to one another and linked
to the fresh-split fence,
their slender budding limbs
and early leaves unfurled
toward the foothills of
the steeper mountains
that I know lie beyond.

Charity

Our distant neighbor wore all of
her departed mother's clothes
layered in remembrance of her
one on top of the other—
sweaters over blouses over skirts over slacks
for insulation against the cold
even during the hottest days of summer

when my mother was the only member
of our parish not to side step her
as she shifted along the sidewalk,
bowed over with her burden of deference,
perspiration dripping in homage
from her hairline and upper lip.

My mother would shunt her own packages,
brush back her windblown bangs,
and momentarily drop my hand
to squeeze Mrs. Gooding's shoulder
and greet her while smiling,
commenting on Sunday's sermon,
asking after her sons.

My own mother now gone,
I am surrounded by a mass
of her unsorted clothes—
they cover the entire bed,
and I have to resist the urge
simply to lie down among them.

I pick up one silk scarf,
then another, wrapping them
around my throat until
I feel my own pulse
beating through.

I slip into her unlaced boots
and momentarily stumble,
taking one step forward,
another back.

I pull on her blue down coat
against the approaching winter,
let her gloves envelop my fingers,
longing for her to return my grasp.

I turn up the collar,
rise to fill the shoulders,
and zip myself in,
then button down
the flaps and cuffs,
allowing myself to delve
into the pockets,
reaching deep
for the strength
of her benevolence
to deliver it over
to charity.

Dear Mom

Well, it turns out
you were right
about everything.
I do regret
every harsh word
ever spoken,
all those family
traditions scorned,
my years of
teenage defiance,
every opportunity missed.
I do yearn for
one more day,
an hour, one more
word with you
the way you did
after Nana died.
I could brew
you a thousand
cups of tea now,
and never tire of
boiling the water,
exacting the proportions
of leaves, sugar, and cream,
ignoring the cautions
of the heart surgeon
if your cup and saucer
would comfort you.
I prepare my own tea
each silent morning,
think of you
with every stir,
sip from the spoon
as if it holds elixir.

What I would give
to bring it to you,
serve it up once more—
this time on a tray
from Nana's silver,
brimming over, but

no burden to deliver,
the polished heirloom pot
shining like a globe.

Who Can Say?

Who can say?
my aunt has jotted beneath
the portrait of a boy—
the white bowed armband
and the gilded bible
he clasps to his chest
signaling his first communion—
Might be your father.
In this one, a woman
with a pale complexion
strikes a formidable pose
beside a dark draped curtain,
but cannot seem to decide
where to place her hands,
as my aunt writes *She's on
my father's side of the family,
but can't say who she is.*
About this beach scene,
composed of a dozen
half-submerged figures
in wool suits and knit caps
squinting into the sun,
she says, *I see only
four who I recognize,
Mom, Dad, my brother, and me.*
Or this spring occasion—
where every woman
dons a corsage,
such an array of hats
and budding branches
it could be Mother's Day or Easter—
Only recognize my cousin here.
Who are they, then,
the ones who stand
shoulder to shoulder
with my kin? Why
have we kept these images
of men and women
who perhaps, only as a courtesy,
delivered their *cartes-de-visites,*
left to permanently reside

within our albums, our company?
We knew them well once,
it seems in some, like this one,
where my aunt sits as a girl
on the lap of a young woman
who embraces her with great affection—
one arm wrapped around my aunt's slight waist,
as the other hand pats her bare knee,
their feet swinging freely beneath them,
though my aunt notes apologetically,
I don't know who is holding me.
It takes me a long while to reconcile
that we will never know now.
My maternal and paternal grandparents,
my mother and father are gone;
only my aunt and uncle remain,
but when I witness
their struggle to
place or label
these blurs of memory,
I cease my inquiries,
and try to allow our reflections
simply to bind and inspire us
to stand before the
query of our own lens,
show future generations
the pose of the past,
leave it to them
to distinguish
one relative
from another,
bestow upon us
our names.

First Illness

This fervent walk
might do us good,
get us away from the fever
of syringe, thermometer, vaporizer,
and serve as my own unwritten prescription
to ease your stifled cure.

I sing through my nerves,
transferring you from car seat to chest pack,
strained lyrics from an enduring lullaby
about longing and loss—fighting
the urge to think the worst.

Slowly, minding every stone and slippery leaf,
I draw you in, finding even footing only
when your brow meets my chin,
and our chests are pressed,
alternating beats of our hearts.

I begin pointing out the prompts
of buds—tiny hands, palms clasped, fingers
poised in a faint green prayer, a scrape
of bark, the rustle of eager squirrels,
a brook spurting its first words,
an arched twig pointing a
crooked way—and then!
one curved twig entwining
with another, nearly braided together,
purely and securely bundled—
tight and frayed with weed—
an entire nest—
nestled and camouflaged—
just a glint of shell at first—and then!
the dappled and blue moody eggs, contoured, whole,
side by each, complete, like fragile promises
smoothing my worry—and then!

I am taken, like a bright page from
a worn storybook, entirely aback by
the vibrant flutter, warm and ruddy,
her beak and wing and claw rising

and descending and rising again—
it is a robin redbreast—

her black eye glossy and piercing
and quick and assured, fierce
in her mission of guarding
this that is her season—
bringing in the spring.

You murmur and curl in
to me as I follow her—
pride and breast expanding,
pumping, rising, emerging skyward,
alighting the top of my head—
my own breath taking flight,
lifting my face, straightening
my neck, pushing my shoulders even—
my arms dropping back and up,
breathing in and exhaling again,
the relief of it, primal, bracing me—

this is how we do it, naturally!
by wrapping, and warming, and rousing, and shielding, and soaring—
nurturing our young through the scourge
of winter, the thorn, the bramble,
from bud to branch to breeze to sky—

clearing in a reflection of myself with you—
my "frost blossom baby"
eternally renewing me

this is where I find it—
your recovery,
imminent.

Leave Taking

My only girl,
all the roads
I've grown to know
with you in the back seat,
aslumber, angelic, aglow.

After our daily story time,
where we'd dance and rhyme,
your imagination teeming
when the hour was done,
your eyelids drooping
with the last round sung,
you'd reach up and we'd quickly depart
from the library, nurture your sleepy mood in the car,
the classical station and a lullaby
soothing you into nap time

while I'd accelerate out of town
in a combination of play and precision,
softly singing while gauging
speed, gas, and traffic signals,
choosing non-stop routes
so as not to disturb you,

deciding on the spur which way to turn,
what road would take us a scenic route,
relying on whim and the weather
to inspire today's destination,
maneuvering the station wagon
into a spot of sun or shade
once we'd finally arrive,

and I'd fold open a map or mothering magazine
in my lap, only to watch you sleep,
feeling fortunate, privileged, singularly blessed
to eye you in the rear-view mirror
as you'd awaken and smile, sing, or giggle,
showing me simply
my contented self
reflected in you.

It is these quiet milestones
I will miss the most
when I return to work
and place you in day care,
no photos or mementos
of the everyday hours we'd share
a thermos or cooler
in the car between us
on suburban adventure
seemingly mundane, common, regular,
but not without its dangers—

the pacified interior of our car,
hushing the anxiety, the urgency
I feel with the passing miles,
each day of my leave I leave behind us,
as if I'm trying to outrun,
within the given limits
of these winding back roads,
the turning of the dashboard clock
sweeping over these moments,
lulling and fleeting—
my steering your childhood
in spontaneous direction,
my heart as compass,
taking the long way,
an open itinerary,
unyielding.

Well, Well, Well

She tried to do well. Every morning, she woke, and rose, and rolled up, and pulled down, and plumped, and smoothed. She filled, and heated, and poured, and sipped, and spooned. She wiped, and selected, and sliced, and spread, wrapped, stacked, packed, folded, zipped, and clipped.

She checked and she tisked and she sang. She flipped, and kissed, and squeezed, and prodded, and fed, urging, brushing, braiding, and buttoning, hoping she was doing well.

She opened, and guided, and tugged, and closed, and latched every latch, and locked. She slid, and buckled, and adjusted, and calmed, and listened, and nodded, and reassured, admiring them in the mirror's rearview.

Daily, she accelerated, braked, signaled, and maneuvered. She pulled evenly in between the lines in the lot every day. She parked and she heard a woman sigh, noticing her own breath escaping, half frozen in the schoolyard air. She turned and she straightened and, as she did daily, she pulled and she tightened and she tucked and she led. Every day, she clasped their hands. She swung their mittens as they, all of them together, walked all the way down the downward hill, one boot, then the other, skipping and scuffing in the snow.

At the double doors, she paused, assuring and advising and praising every day. She nodded and some days she winked. Every day, she kissed. She patted and then, bracing, taking one step back, then another, she parted. Although she did it daily, she always faltered at this turning away. She waved again. Then again, she waved. She blew kisses, one flutter, then the other—the snow falling between them.

She walked uphill then, one foot, then the other heavy boot following. She pulled the door handle, and swung and shut and looked ahead. She occupied the driver's seat. She adjusted her watch, and strained to listen, and tried to fill that silence with radio song. She reversed, she turned the wheel, and she signaled, wondering if there was a way to know if today she had done well.

Well, she went on trying to do well. She shopped and chopped and stocked their cupboards every day. Daily, she drove and she loaded and unloaded the station wagon fairly well as she did well, every day.

Every day, she thought of everything. Well, almost everything every day. Anything she forgot, well, she hoped it was forgotten. Daily, she did well at biding her time, every day waiting to be well on her way.

Then she was there, where she found herself every day, at the top of the hill, this day lingering, standing, arms crossed, elbows cupped in her palms, to take in today, this day, today, in which she thought she had done reasonably well. The bell rings and releases her successes—suddenly rushing toward her, now, in succession, scarf fringe and smiles flying, calling out, their greetings rebounding the playing ground, proving she had done well—very well. Well, well, well.

Orbit

My daughter wrestles,
with great clamor, a meteor
down from the dark
before breakfast,
inquisitive, triumphant,
and unharmed.

After the breaking of
dawn, she chomps,
with budding teeth
and swollen gums,
on the moon—
exploring its craters
with all ten fingers
as she contemplates,
drools, and chews.

On impulse, she shakes
Saturn free of its rings,
grabs at the center
of the sun, stretches
out its rays, and,
in a snap, allows them
to bounce back—
spinning and rattling the globe,
the mobile, and
our whole morning
into motion—

in the unfurling daylight,
she snatches suspended birds
mid-flight—temporarily enraptured
by their chiming cries
before, with a shove,
dismissing the flock,

propelling them on
in order to watch their wings
as they again resume motion—
the up and down,
the forward and back,

mollifying, for a moment,
her capricious impatience

before she turns to grasp
and clap the startled
stars together, and
in a whim of invention,
there is light
as she sets them off
singing and twinkling
with a big bang!

She is six-months old,
this fair-haired,
saucer-eyed,
pink-cheeked
force of nature,
yet there is nothing
infantile about her—

in fact, I find her infinitely wise
in her desire to grasp
and possess all the life
within reach around her—
intent on simultaneously
rendering and soothing
the blessings and curses
she bestows and utters
at the center of my world—

the axis at which
we are aligned—
from where I listen for,
from where I look upon,
from where I encompass
and try to guide her—
only to suddenly,
humbly find, and
gratefully see as
I am circling her,
she is orbiting me.

Author's Note:

My mother lived a long and remarkable life, but I could never persuade her to complete a memoir. Toward the end of her life she said to me simply, "You write it."

My mother sought comfort in the familiar after my father died by maintaining our family home, and in the process she instilled in me the importance of daily ritual. Her presence throughout my childhood inhabited much of the space my father's absence created; nevertheless, when I began to write creatively as a young girl, I thought that gift was given to me by my father, from a holy and divine place in Heaven.

When I grew up and moved away, learning to sustain myself and persevere in the outside world, my mother's letters about her home life served as a touchstone for me, making a great and lasting impression. I realized it was she who taught me to value and explore in my writing everyday domestic practices and draw on them for inspiration and lifelong balance.

One of the ways I honor her legacy is to write about mothering my own daughters. When they are upset, it is my voice, my touch, my rock and sway, and my scent that allows me to pacify them. In turn, they make me feel like a gentle deity or a maternal heroine. Trusting my every instinct about their care has made me stronger, more confident, and, thus far, invincible.

My daughters do not yet know the qualities they have instilled in me, but with each reach and every inclination toward me, they sustain me, lift me, teach me, and prepare me to be their mother and a better woman beyond.

Megeen R. Mulholland has a keen interest in the intersection of literature and art. She relishes the experience of sorting through dilapidated attic boxes, peeling apart glossies and negatives, and bending back curled corners of proofs as she explores her family's snapshot photography. For her, poetry is a way of transcribing visual images and rendering literary snapshots of her extended Irish family.

She often incorporates snapshots in the text of her poems, creating a dialogue between oral narrative and images and drawing parallels between the fleeting nature of the act of photography and that of life.

She incorporates these insights in all types of writing, including poetry, fiction, creative non-fiction, and book reviews, which have appeared in a wide range of anthologies, literary magazines, and academic journals.

She has delivered academic papers, including "Proof: Ekphrasis and Snapshot Photography" and "Unposing the American Family Portrait," and served on panels at a wide array of conferences, from the University of Louisville in Kentucky to Ryerson University in Toronto, Ontario.

Dr. Mulholland received her Ph.D. from the University at Albany where she received Honorable Mention in the Eugene K. Garber Prize for Short Fiction. She is also a graduate of the Master of Arts program in English and Creative Writing at Binghamton University. She is currently an Associate Professor at Hudson Valley Community College where she teaches literature and creative writing and is engaged in the Campus Poetry Project.

www.ingramcontent.com/pod-product-compliance
Lightning Source LLC
LaVergne TN
LVHW050045090426
835510LV00043B/3200